Charde Vera

Nayomi Montes

He Is

Library of congress: 2023900655

ISBN: 979-8-9885294-0-8 (Hardcover)
ISBN: 978-1-7374173-8-5 (Paperback)

Website: www.chardevera.com
Email: info@chardevera.com

Dedications

To my son Noah and my nephews Christian, Ishmael and Akeem Jr I love you! You are so important and loved, remember to believe and trust in yourselves always!

To every boy! To say you are strong, brave, unique, and smart is one thing, but to believe it for yourself is everything! Keep on believing! Keep on trusting! Keep on loving yourselves always!

He uses his abilities, putting them to the test.
He smiles knowing he did his very best.

What does being gifted mean to you?

HE IS GIFTED.

He does right by everyone when he makes deals,
and shows himself to be genuine and real.

What does being honest mean to you?

HE IS HONEST.

Forgiveness is a gift that he's willing to give
because he knows it's a wonderful way to live.

What does being forgiving mean to you?

HE IS FORGIVING.

He will impress you with his awesome love
and always strives to reach above.

What does being awesome mean to you?

HE IS AWESOME.

He has courage and self-belief. He has a spirit of power.
Helping him stay ready and brave so he may never cower.

What does being courageous mean to you?

HE IS COURAGEOUS.

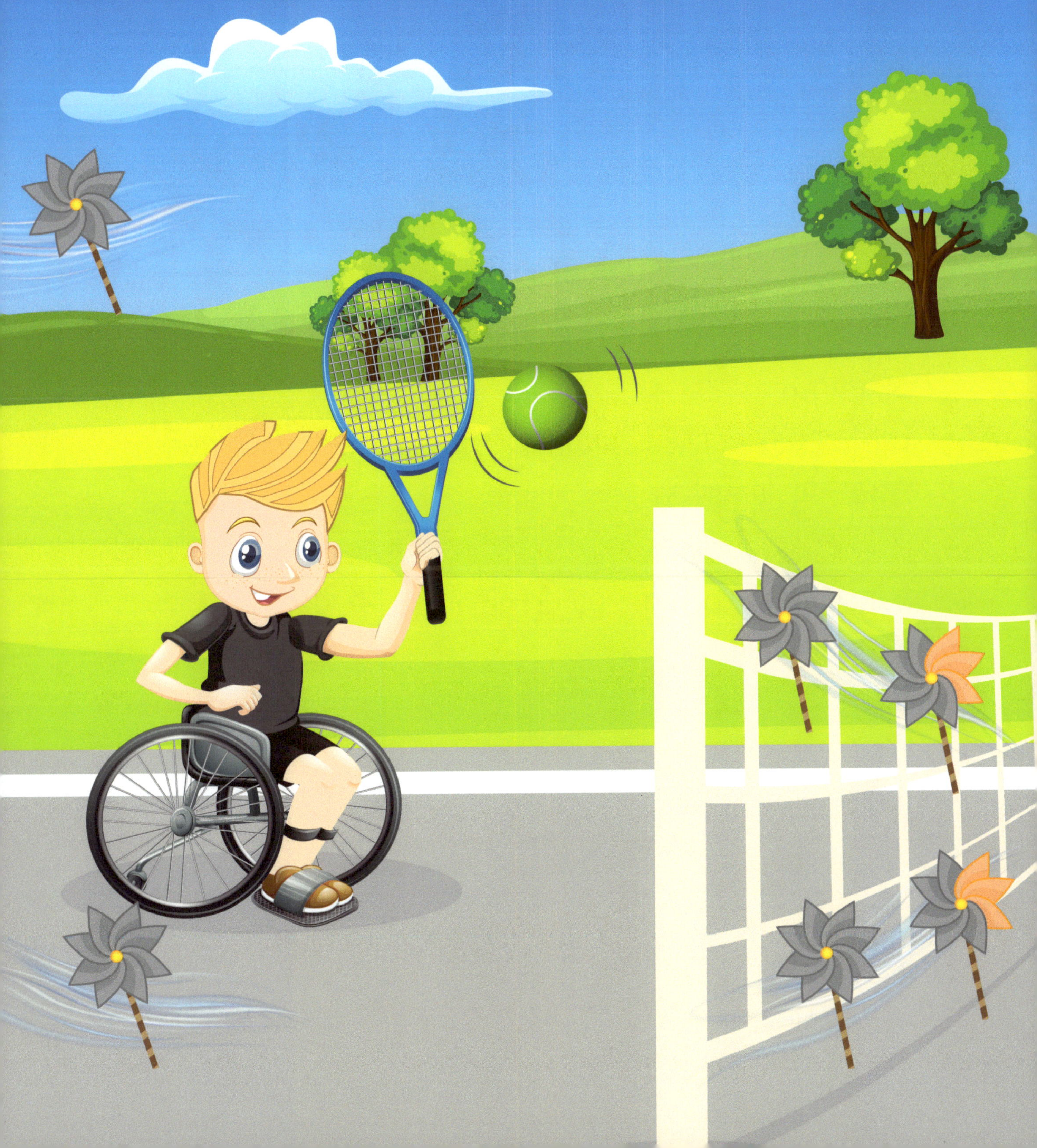

He is powerful not because he has the greatest strength,
but because the knowledge in his heart can reach amazing lengths.

What does being powerful mean to you?

HE IS POWERFUL.

He has faith that will last a lifetime, and hope that will carry him through.
He is special because he is always kind, positive, warm and funny too.

What does being special mean to you?

HE IS SPECIAL.

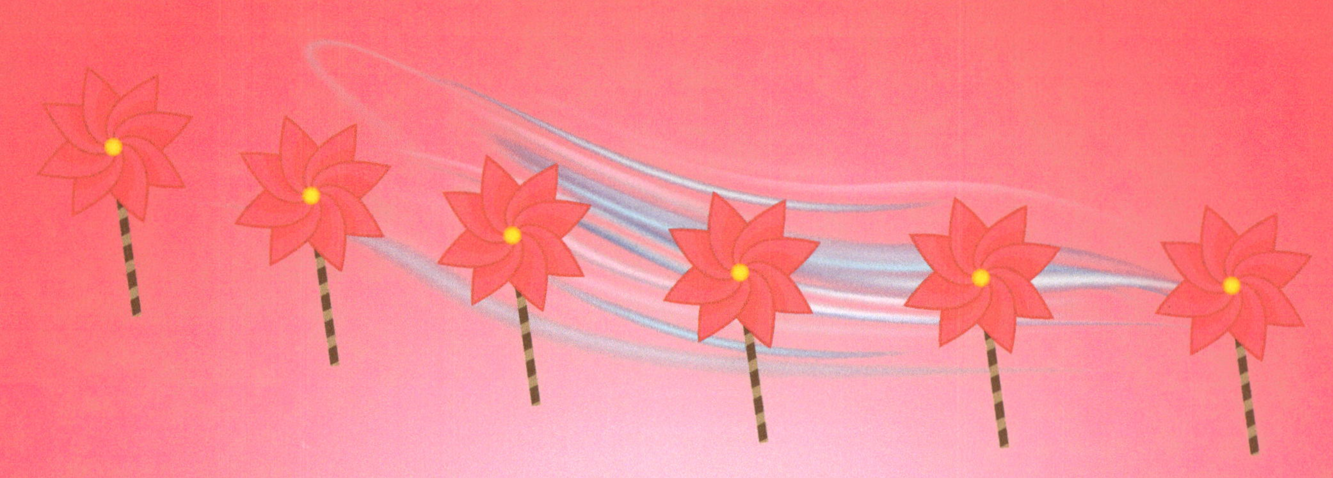

He is cooler than a snowy day, and his personality is so chill.
He is always willing to laugh and play and has confidence in his skill.

What does being cool mean to you?

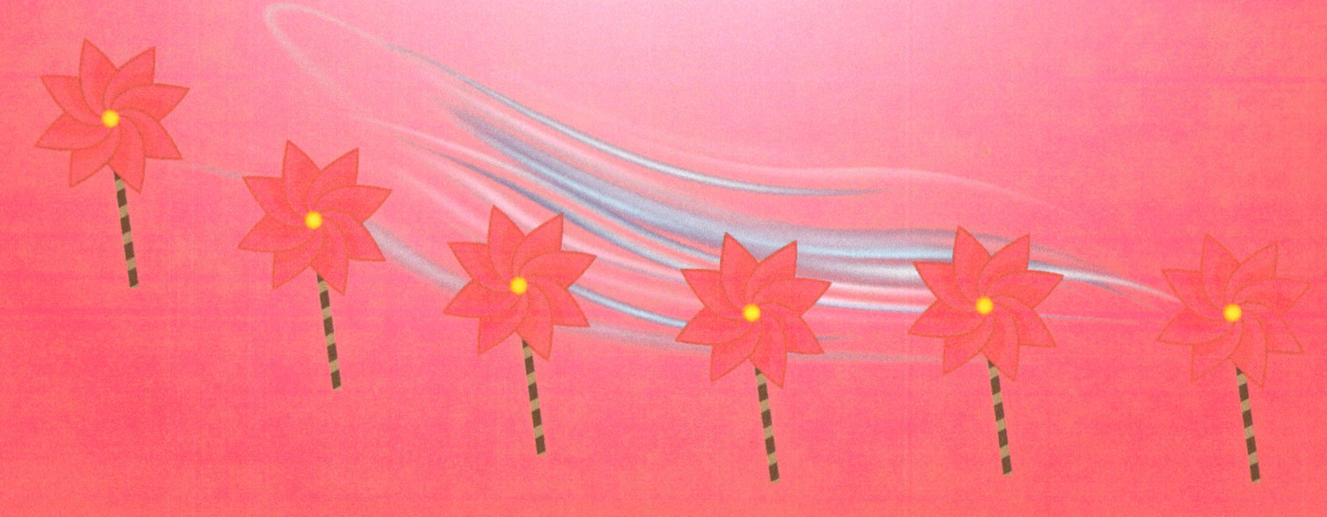

HE IS COOL.

He is thankful and sweet, with an appreciative attitude.
Because of this humility he always shows gratitude.

What does being grateful mean to you?

HE IS GRATEFUL.

He is a delightful person from his head to his toes.
He is admired by all the people he knows.
He is positive in all the right ways,
and has confidence that he always displays.

What does being wonderful mean to you?

HE IS WONDERFUL.

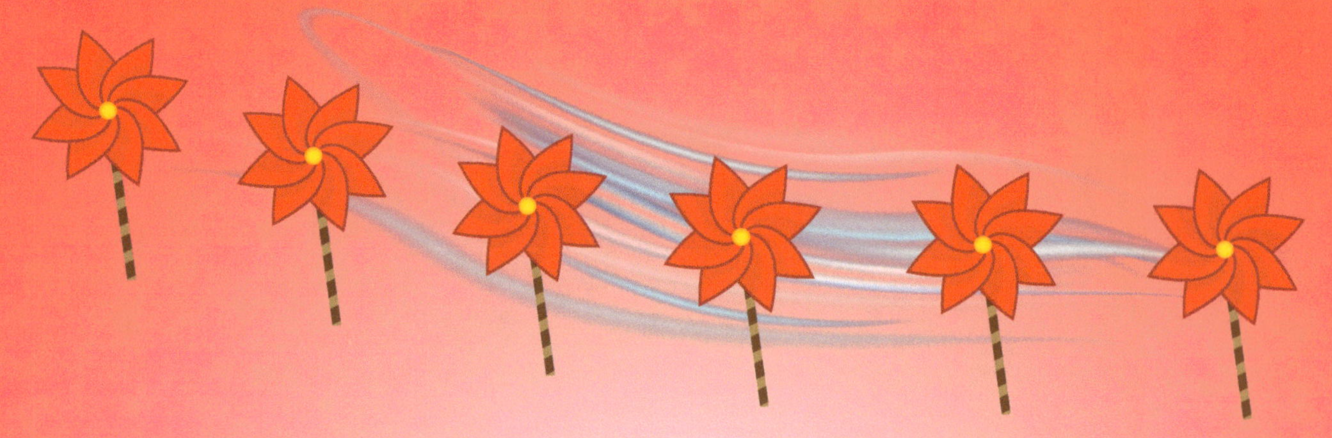

He is pleasant, friendly, helpful, and so kind.
He charms all he meets with his positive mind.

What does being charming mean to you?

HE IS CHARMING.

He can handle all problems and stay calm and cool.
He will never let impatience make him be a fool.

What does being patient mean to you?

HE IS PATIENT.

He is me. He Is you.
He is us.

We are important
We are worthy
We matter.

Charde Vera is a certified life coach, author, US Navy veteran, loving wife, and mother who has been passionate about writing and journaling from a very young age. As a budding and publishing author, Charde has written a journal titled, "I Am" and co-authored a transformational book called "Radical Woman." Following on the success of her book, "She Is," Charde's latest book, "He Is," is also co-illustrated by her daughter, Nayomi, a children's poetry affirmation book that encourages children to trust love and believe in themselves. She captures her young readers' minds with an artistic writing style that is simple, easily understandable, and with a smooth flow. Through her books, Charde provides children with a platform to enable them to express their feelings and get out of their comfort zone.

She believes that words are important and that how we speak into and over our lives sets the foundation for our future. Charde reminds people that they are worthy and valuable. Her soft spot for children has seen her create awareness by nurturing the minds of young adults through her words and feeding them with positivity that will go a long way to transform and inspire their lives.

When she is not working on her next literary works, Charde enjoys spending time with her family, reading, vlogging, and traveling with her family.

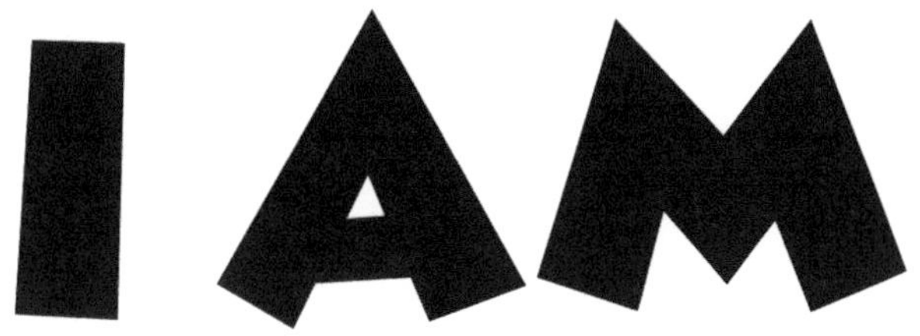

I AM Patient because

I AM Honest because

I AM Forgiving because

I AM Awesome because

I AM Courageous because

I AM Special because

I AM Cool because

I AM Grateful because

I AM Wonderful because

I AM Charming because

I AM Gifted because

I AM Powerful because

www.ingramcontent.com/pod-product-compliance
Lightning Source LLC
Chambersburg PA
CBHW042051100726
47973CB00014B/213

9798988529408